MY AMAZING LIFE

IN WORDS AND PICTURES

BY

BRIAN WILLIAMS

1. First things first

2. My life outside school

3. Starting out in the big wide world

4. My life is turned upside down

5. How I started in business

6. An unusual wedding

7. How I progressed in life

8. Absolutely terrible

9. Travelling man

10. Retirement

11. A real retirement

FIRST THINGS FIRST

My name is Brian Williams, and I was born in Hemel Hempstead, Hertfordshire, on December 30th 1941, a war baby. I was the eldest child of Gwen and Harry Williams. I had two brothers and a sister, David, Anthea and Martin who followed in that order. I was born at West Herts Hospital, the back entrance to that property being fifty yards from my parent's home on the same road, Maynard Road.

Brian and mum.

However, one part of a normal family was missing. By the time I was three years old, I didn't have any grandparents, and my brothers David and Martin, along with my sister Anthea, never knew their grandparents at all. Can you imagine not knowing your grandmother or grandfather at all?

It was not until I started school and was talking to the children in the playground that I found out what grandparents were. My mum and dad had married late in life, and my mum was forty years old when I was born, their parents were quite old to start with, and people did not live to the age they do today.

My father did not enjoy the best of health and we all lived a very basic life with mum at the helm of a very happy home in Beechfield Road, Boxmoor.

Before Hemel Hempstead became a new town, I lived in Boxmoor Village on a new council estate, and the village centre had all the shops we needed. I would be left in my pram, with all the others, outside the shops, while mum popped in.

There was an electrical shop where toasters, kettles and televisions, for the few people that had one, went to be mended.

Mr Mansbridge had a family baker's shop, and delivered bread by horse and cart. Hot cross buns were brought round on Good Friday.

At the greengrocers, fruit and veg would be weighed and tipped into your shopping bag, so everything was muddled together.

There was a great village feeling which has been lost today, especially with the advent of the supermarket that has taken over local shopping and eroded local community life.

Aged around two and a half.

Brian and David

As I grew up, my instinct would take me to the top of our back garden, and through a hole in the fence. and half way down an embankment covered in trees. At the bottom was a single railway line where a steam engine would haul passenger coaches from Boxmoor to Harpenden. Seeing this was the highlight of any day until my Dad found out.

Brian, David and baby Anthea

Admiring the tree.

I remember really enjoying Christmas as I grew up, and was really excited when I knew Father Christmas was coming down the chimney to leave a present for me. Back in 1947 having a present was something special, especially when it came from Father Christmas.

I didn't really enjoy school, and although I had reasonable intelligence it was always a struggle. I do remember my parents finding the money for me to have a five-day school holiday to St Mary's Bay holiday camp at Dymchurch in Kent. This was the first holiday without my family.

You may remember the Eleven-plus exam at primary school, which decided whether you went to the grammar or the secondary school. In my case, I went to the latter. I passed the maths exam but failed English.

So that was that, Brian went to Corner Hall Secondary School, commonly known as the Prison on the Hill. It was situated at the top of a big hill. The lower part of the school was for the girls and the upper part inhabited by the boys.

When I started there, I walked to and from school which was about two miles each way, no buses then. After a couple of years, I went by bike and pushed it up the hill, there were no gears on my cycle at that time. I spent one year getting up before 6.00am to collect and deliver newspapers.

Although the school was all one building, there was no way the boys could meet the girls, as there were separate playgrounds. Discipline was very strict. All the teachers would have a stick at their desk. The stick was used a lot, including on me. A rap across the knuckles really hurt. One of my disadvantages at school was that I didn't have a good memory. I was in the A stream but usually near the bottom. I always thought it would be better to be at the top in the B stream. But I persevered, and finally was more than happy to leave school when I was still only 14 years of age. This school was demolished many years ago and the land is now a housing estate with a large Tesco store.

A happy childhood.

MY LIFE OUTSIDE SCHOOL

When I was growing up, being a child was a totally different experience from what it is today. Life was so much simpler. We made our own entertainment as our parents were not in a position for us to attend anything that cost money. It was just an enjoyable, easy going, stress-free life. There wasn't much traffic and it was easy to get about and meet lovely people that appreciated life.

I was also a boy scout. I remember taking part in bob-a-job week, where scouts would help local people with chores such as gardening, car washing, dog walking or shopping, and get a shilling, which is 5p in today's money. Because I loved gardening and was very good at digging, I got those jobs. But the scout leader thought people were taking advantage of me and cut down my activities a bit.

From the age of about nine, I enjoyed travelling and seeing our wonderful countryside. I remember visiting my Uncle George and Auntie Ness a number of times, which was a long trip. It involved walking half a mile to a bus stop on the A41, which at the time was the main road from London to Birmingham. It's hard to believe now how light the traffic was, even though the M1 had not yet been built.

I travelled on the Green Line Coach, which was an express service running from London to Aylesbury. I stayed on the coach for about sixteen miles, then got a local bus from the bus station to Grendon Underwood, a small village where my auntie and uncle lived. They had an old detached house with a large orchard on the other side of the road.

Needless to say, on leaving, weighed down with a heavy bag of apples, I was always pleased to see the local bus arrive to return me to Aylesbury and the Green Line coach home.

The fact that I could complete this journey alone at such a young age just shows how different life was for children then. You wouldn't let a nine-year-old set off on a thirty-mile bus journey now, and with a change of buses in the middle, too.

A few years after my visits, Grendon Underwood became very famous for the wrong reasons. An experimental type of prison was built on the edge of the village, with a psychiatric unit for prisoners with antisocial personal disorders. It slowly evolved into a mainstream prison, but is still the only one of its kind in the country, being a therapeutic prison community for treating sex offenders and seriously violent inmates.

I also enjoyed the bus journey from Hemel Hempstead to St. Albans. There was the added interest of open countryside though half way there, the bus had to be careful going over a large new road bridge, underneath which the M1 motorway was being constructed.

I also went to my first concert at the Odeon Cinema there

- March 9th 1958 - to see the one and only, top of the bill, Lonny Donegan and his Skiffle Group. How times have changed.

I saw Lonnie Donegan at the Odeon in 1958.

One of the things I really enjoyed was going with, or seeing, my friends, on the bridge which was over the main railway line between London Euston and Glasgow. This was situated south of the local Hemel Hempstead railway station, and was formerly known as Boxmoor Station. The railway line was very busy and I used to love watching the steam trains thundering along, and the slower steam hauled freight trains. I found it so fascinating with all the different types of steam engines and their capacity to travel at such high speeds.

It was no surprise I became a train spotter, and because of that I travelled to many other locations to see different types of locomotives that operated in other areas of the railway network. This was all very wonderful except for one thing. I needed money to follow my dream.

It is interesting to note that when I was a boy it was quite easy to obtain part-time work to earn some pocket money. This was mainly newspaper rounds or Saturday shop work. I managed to get a job as a newspaper delivery boy at Woods, the local newsagents. At that time, every household had a paper delivered, and mark my words, the newspapers were thick. School regulations stipulated that you had to be 13 years of age and were not allowed to deliver before seven in the morning. My delivery round was about 70 newspapers each day, most of which were delivered before I went to school and the rest on the way to school, for the princely sum of seven shillings for the week's work. This would be 35p in new money and worth £6.70 today. This got a bit much, so one day I asked for a rise in pay and was promptly shown the door. Bye, Brian.

After a little while I managed to get a casual job working for Byron's the chemist. I delivered medicines to customers who were not able to get to the shop. I used the shop bicycle which had a metal square attached to the front of the handlebars to put the medicines in, and off I pedalled, delivering the goods. This included a three-mile trip to a village called Bovingdon, which is at the top of a long, high hill. Needless to say, I was glad when this job ended.

I had one more job on a Saturday morning which I really enjoyed. This was working for Earls, the butcher, earning half a crown per day (two shillings and sixpence or 12½p - £2.30 today) plus 2lb of sausages for my mum. Most of my work involved cycling the butchers' bike delivering joints of meat to customers on the new housing estate called Chaulden, which was about a mile away. Can you imagine having meat delivered to you on a bicycle? Health and safety was not invented in those days. It was an old fashioned butcher's shop, and they bought cattle on a Wednesday morning at Tring cattle market. These would be delivered the next day to the shop where there was a large yard and slaughter house at the back. I found this really interesting but won't go into the gruesome details – or maybe just one story to show how different things were before health and safety was invented.

A lady came into the shop one Saturday before Christmas for her order – a large chicken.   The chicken was not sold oven-ready, I had to go out into the yard and catch it.
It was taken to the slaughter house, had its head and tail removed, was plucked and had its innards and the giblets removed. It was then washed, taken into the shop all wrapped up in paper, and what happened, the paper was rustling as if it was still alive. It was unbelievable.

All this gave me some pocket money. It also taught me that working hard doesn't do you any harm, and helped me prepare for the next big step in my life.

I hope you are enjoying reading about my life, as it is not all about being clever, but more importantly about having your head screwed on and learning to cope with what life throws at you, in my case an awful lot.

I did a lot of cycling in those days.

STARTING OUT IN THE BIG WIDE WORLD

As I have mentioned, I left school at 14 with nothing to show for it – no exam passes or qualifications. I left as the Christmas holidays started, being two weeks away from my 15th birthday. In those days there was no such thing as further education.

My interest in the railways made me think about looking for a job with British Rail. On my 15th birthday, in 1956, I started work as a junior porter at Berkhamsted railway station. I remember my very first task was helping to unload soaking wet boxes of fish from a goods train. The area also had a lot of watercress beds. I would handle loads of wet chips (boxes) every day, which had to be stacked in piles according to their destinations. All this had to be done in six minutes while the train waited. Another of my delicate commodities came from Dwight's Pheasantries, a large supplier of pheasants' eggs.

At this time, as a station porter, I had a busy workload because everything was delivered by train. There were no lorries or vans travelling up and down motorways – there wouldn't even be motorways until 1958 – so the railways were a very important link in getting goods to and from shops and factories. This also included mail trains transporting parcels and letters all over the country. A mail bag was not light.

The station had its share of local passenger trains, mainly between London Euston and Bletchley, with a few continuing to Wolverton and Northampton. Milton Keynes railway station did not exist. It was all just nice open countryside with a few small villages. One of the things that attracted people to Berkhamsted on the train was Champneys health resort for rich people to come and stay for a while. For me this was wonderful. When passengers alighted from the train I would carry their cases outside to a taxi, and if I was lucky I might even get a shilling, which is worth about 87p now. As I was earning only about £3 (about £52 these days) a week, the tip was a lot of money to me.

I had been at Berkhamsted station as a junior porter for about nine months when I was told of a vacancy for a junior booking clerk at Boxmoor Station (now Hemel Hempstead). This was my dream. I was always very envious of the man in the booking office at Berkhamsted, and this new position was also nearer to my home.

With my limited experience working on the railway and meeting the general public, I was over the moon when I got the position. I really worked hard learning about the job. The more I worked, the more I loved it. If you really enjoy your work, it becomes easy to be good at it and in this respect I was offered a change in my working conditions. Apsley was the next station from Boxmoor going towards London. Only a few trains stopped there, so the booking clerk at Boxmoor worked at both stations. As Apsley station got busier, I moved there as the permanent booking clerk.

At that time, the largest employer in Hemel Hempstead was John Dickinson & Co, a large paper mill employing thousands of people. It was situated at Apsley, on the edge of Hemel Hempstead. The company had arranged with BR to have a station built for their employees. One of my jobs was to read the gas and electric meters. The gas meter was alongside the main line in a hut which really smelled of gas. I also had to read the water meter. This was taken from a drain on the edge of the main road (the old A41) very close to where you leave the station. The electric meter was indoors at the station. As the town expanded and became designated by the government as a new town, passenger numbers became much greater which meant more trains stopping at Apsley.

MY LIFE IS TURNED UPSIDE DOWN

From the day I started work I really enjoyed it, and looked forward to many happy years working for British Rail at the booking office, but little did I know what was coming to change the rest of my life.

As I mentioned, I loved my job working at Apsley. It was like being my own boss. I had total control over the running of the station. This involved issuing tickets, keeping accounts, checking and ordering stock, collecting and checking tickets from alighting passengers, and helping them with their luggage and parcels. I had no idea that at 17 years of age, a dramatic moment that happened to me in the booking office would change my life forever.

I was in the office serving a customer at the window which I had done so many times before. I looked up to pull out a single ticket to London Euston from the rack (no electronic issue of tickets in those days), and the next minute was unconscious on the floor. An ambulance was called and I woke up in the West Herts hospital. Apparently, I had had an epileptic fit.

Nothing like this had ever happened to me, or to any member of my family, before. There was no medical record whatsoever. When I woke up, I was very dizzy as my head had repeatedly banged on the floor during my fit. The hospital did what they needed to sort me out.

Without my knowledge, although I was 17 years old, and nothing mentioned to me, or to my parents, I was transferred to Hill End Hospital for Mental and Nervous Diseases in St Albans. During the 1950s, epilepsy was considered to be a mental illness.

My father was not happy, to say the least, when he came to collect me the next morning. Hill End was a terrible and violent place to be. Very aggressive patients were placed there, and it was an absolute nightmare for me to see this, something I had no experience of, and have never forgotten since.

Once home, I was making a good recovery. The prescribed medication worked well, and the hospital advised certain procedures to follow if or when it happened again. A week later, while I was recuperating at home, something happened which these days is illegal.

A letter arrived from British Rail terminating my employment with immediate effect. My father and I went up to their head office in London to request that I should keep my job and to explain the circumstances. It was clearly pointed out to us in no uncertain terms that because not enough research had been done into epilepsy it was considered a mental problem and there was no chance of me keeping my job. No other job offer would be made to me now or at any time in the future. This was a real shock to me. All this had plainly told me that my medical condition was not a very nice one. I had lost my dream job and had no idea what the future would hold in life. To say things looked bleak would be an understatement.

Eventually, I decided that this wasn't going to hold me back, and over the next few years I found I had no problem in finding other jobs. This included working for a travel agent, and also working as an office clerk in different companies. I had a number of jobs because of having fits and partial fits. But I continued being employed, learning more about epilepsy, keeping my medication under control and knowing what to do when medical problems occurred. I also learned not to worry about it too much and keep relaxed. My social life was greatly restricted, but altogether enjoyable especially when involved with my sister and two brothers. I have not forgotten the full support I received from my parents.

We were all involved in a local scooter club (not connected in any way with the mods and rockers of those days). The club organised visits to many different scootering events by other clubs in the country. One such event was a five-a-side football tournament at Nottingham. We were all having a great time, but many of us weren't used to this energetic sport, me included. I am not sure what happened next in this somewhat skilled game, but I was tackled and hit the ground. I had to be taken to Nottingham hospital where I had confirmation that my leg was broken in two places (tibia and fibula). I was told it was a bad break. They tried to straighten the bone, which again is something that I have never forgotten. This procedure failed, and I was left for two days with a broken bone in a side ward. All I could see, while lying in bed, looking up through the window, was a brick wall. If I had been able to look straight out, I would have been able to see scantily clad ladies playing tennis.

I was then informed that I was being transferred to West Herts hospital in Hemel Hempstead. Now, bearing in mind the lack of health and safety legislation in those days, the following transfer procedure took place: a nurse and ambulance staff arrived and I was placed on a stretcher with a blanket, and taken to Nottingham railway station. With me on a stretcher, they placed it on a porter's flat barrow and wheeled me into the station, then up in a lift and to the appropriate platform. I was given a cup of tea while lying on the wheelbarrow waiting for the train. When the train arrived, the stretcher was laid at an angle across a reserved compartment and a male nurse came with me. Luckily this was the fast train to St Pancras. On arrival in London, an ambulance was waiting for me, and I was driven the fifty miles to West Herts hospital in Hemel Hempstead. The nurse then caught the next train back to Nottingham.

I had an operation to insert a metal plate into my leg to repair the broken bones. That plate is still in place today.

After spending a week in hospital, I returned home on crutches. There was plenty of time ahead of me to think about my life and which way would it go from here. I felt it was going from bad to worse.

The one positive thing in this whole episode was that fact that I still had a job. I was working for Hawker Sidley Dynamics at Hatfield, as a bought ledger clerk. This was checking invoices and passing them on for payment. All paper and bookwork, no computers at this point in time.

Not long after returning to work, I remember making payment for an invoice in respect of a job advert for a computer operator at HSD at Stevenage. I thought to myself "I could do this!" I went outside to the phone box during my lunch break. Being the same company it was easy for them to make enquiries, and lo and behold, a week later I got the job. It was more money, but permanent night shift. This was quite good as it was a 10-hour shift Monday night to Thursday night, which meant I had a long weekend.

It was in the very early days of the computer industry. The input was punched cards which were loaded and stored on tapes. This took time to produce the information required, which included the company payroll, unlike how it is today.

I remember one night I was working on producing

the company payroll and wage packets. We always had a look at the main print-out to see what wages we were going to get. I was horrified to see everybody was paying double tax. It turned out the lead card, showing the tax number, was punched wrong. I had to cancel everything and start again with a new lead card. The boss came to work at 9.00am and we were half way through the payroll, say no more.

It was an interesting job, it enabled me to save some money, and my health was much better. After a year I made a bold decision – I gave in my notice. My boss and friends at work thought I had gone mad. I was doing a job I loved, and then to give notice, especially after all I'd been through. I fully agreed with them – but what had I decided to do?

During my time at work I did not see my boss, Mr Jackson, very often, except in special circumstances, or emergency. This was because my night shift finished before he started work in the mornings. When giving in my notice I did so in writing and left the note on his desk before I went home. It's always nice when you don't see your boss very often. It makes work easier and more enjoyable, apart from the fact that I did not like people telling me what to do. Mr Jackson was the type of boss who worried a lot. I remember going on holiday abroad during the summer and purchasing a gift for him – a set of worry beads!

Needless to say, my boss was in early the morning after my resignation and called me to his office.

"I am sorry you are leaving. There is no mention in your letter about why you are leaving. Is everything all right?" he asked.

"Yes, thanks," I said.

He asked if I had a new and better job. I told him I had no job to go to, but I had decided to become self-employed. It was then I mentioned that for the last two months during my long weekends I had been a part-time market trader selling household linen, which had been very enjoyable. The system for non-regular traders was to turn up at the market early before it started. If there were any spare stalls not taken up by the regular traders, we could set up our stalls. If not, we had to go home.

I went self-employed to become a permanent market trader, with a vision of having my own shop.

HOW I STARTED IN BUSINESS

To say that my life never runs smoothly is an understatement, and it was about to get much tougher and more unpredictable, especially with thinking about starting a retail business. The following is an insight into how I started and how I progressed.

I have always had an organising brain. I remember when I was walking along the High Street asking myself how did the small shops build up and become a profitable business? How did the shop owner arrive at the point on what to sell? Everybody had to start from scratch, how did they do it? This really fascinated me.

Basically, I left school at 14 with no qualifications. I had my illness under control with medication and thought I'd have a go at being self-employed. At the time, in my estimation, it was worth taking a chance with a reasonable degree of success, bearing in mind a supermarket was unheard of then. After working permanent nights for a year, and doing casual market trading, my social life had gone out of the window. But it enabled me to save some money and take a gamble. As far as I was concerned I had nothing to lose, but I had the challenge of a lifetime.

Then came the nitty gritty. What was I going to sell? Obviously, it had to be something that people would want to buy on a regular basis and to give me a living.

However, if there was a retail shop not selling anything that was needed by the general public, why had somebody else not thought of it? My intention was not to make a fortune, but to enjoy myself and make a reasonable living. There is nothing like working for yourself, because you create your own destiny.

It was not too difficult to decide what to sell as I had been selling household linens on a market stall whilst still at work. Through a trade publication called The Market Trader, I rented an indoor market space at the new Elephant and Castle shopping centre in south London. The shopping centre was a new development with the market area in a very good position, as it was next to the thoroughfare for people using the railway station. When the big day came that I started trading it was understandably very quiet. However, I was able to have a good chat with a fellow trader. I enquired what the previous tenant used to sell. His reply was "dress remnants". I had never heard of them.

Trade was slow at the shopping centre. At this point I got in touch with a friend of mine, whose wife was good at dressmaking. I was not, however, in a position to employ anyone. But after talks, we went into partnership, this being a legal and binding agreement, and a name for the business was required, plus registration with the appropriate authorities. After a lot of thought, we decided to name the business Equality – a man and a woman working together.

Despite the introduction of dress remnants alongside the household linen, trade was still slow. I found out that all the terraced houses along the Old Kent Road had been flattened to make way for a huge development of flats. The problem was that the shopping centre had been completed but the flats were not yet ready for occupation. This created a lack of footfall – a shop keepers' term for not many customers.

As my money was running low, I decided to take up the option printed in my contract – finishing the tenancy after three months. During this time, I was lucky enough to rent a small lock up shop from the council, which included an unusable one bed flat, for a £500 premium and low rent. The shop was located in a small shopping parade in Apsley, Hemel Hempstead. The shop was on the main A41 road going to Watford. This was my last throw of the dice. I was really worried with the all or nothing situation. I was finding out the hard way how to continue my own business. However, I was very determined but everything was hinging on a good bank manager!

Whilst my partner, Sandy, was working at the Elephant and Castle shopping centre, I was at the shop sorting the grubby place out and getting it ready for trading. I am not a DIY man, and I was drilling holes to fix shelving brackets on the wall when I went straight through an electrical cable which bent the drill and sent me off the ladder on to the floor. I was not aware that the floor was concrete or that there were electrical cables behind the wall. This taught me a big lesson and I was lucky to live to tell the tale.

I acquired most of the shop fittings from a skip outside British Home Stores at Harrow. They were refurbishing the store and throwing out all the old units, which was very convenient. One Saturday, I moved the shop stock which was still household linen and dress remnants, to my shop in Apsley. This was while my partner was at the shop sorting everything out. The next day we both went to Salford, Manchester. The journey was very different then as the M1 finished at the Derby turn off.

We went there to purchase dress remnants from a wholesale fabric warehouse which I had found through a trade magazine. When our shop opened, the plan was to sell off the household linen stock and concentrate on the dress remnants with the appropriate accessories. As the shop was in a secondary shopping area, a specialist approach was the way forward.

To make any shop viable, the customer required a very good selection of goods sold. To achieve this there must be a good stockholding, and most important, any shop must cater for changes in customer requirements. In my case, this was being aware of changes in fashion. To do this, and to try and build up the business on a limited budget, it was most important to get to know the customers and purchase the right stock. I could not afford to make mistakes. It was like walking on a tightrope. I would drive to Manchester once a week and purchase dress remnants to keep the stock changing and obtain demand stock to build the business up and keep customers coming to the shop. After a few months trading, there were two developments that changed the course of my business life.

As mentioned, my shop was in a secondary area of Hemel Hempstead called Apsley. I was totally unaware that the government of the day had made Apsley an improvement area which meant they had made a grant to the local council. This involved the empty flat above my shop which was uninhabitable, and the rear part of the shop that had no access to the flat. As money was allocated, the work on my council property was completed in two months. I was presented with a slightly larger shop, with an internal staircase and a wonderful one-bedroom flat. All it cost me was an increase in the rent, or did it?!

During the trading period before the building work, my business partner dropped a bombshell. Because of all the work involved, and the long hours, she came to the conclusion that it was too much to commit herself to the business, and no longer wished to be a partner. Then came the sting in the tail, she demanded a £1000 buy out figure. This was the sum her financial advisor had recommended, taking into account the value of the lease when the new building work was completed. This was out of the question, as all my money was tied up in the business. Obviously I needed every penny to build up the stock holding. With a situation like this I was in danger of losing my dream through no fault of my own. It would have been devastating in the circumstances.

In an attempt to save the business, I made arrangements to see my bank manager, and also got an appointment with a solicitor specialising in partnerships. Thankfully, quite quickly an agreement was reached which was £500 compensation, plus the legal costs of £200 for which I arranged a loan agreed by my bank manger after long negotiations and stipulations. It is interesting to be aware, having a partner is a good way for two people working together in building a business without the financial outlay for staff wages, however, as with my experience, with the best will in the world a partnership is a very dangerous game. The outcome at this stage was that I was on my own and could either sink or swim.

The reality of the situation sunk into my mind very quickly. I was self-employed, without a guaranteed income, very little capital and no staff. I also knew very little about my core business, the dress remnants. In this respect, I took a crash course in dressmaking and the different types of fabric available that were needed to make different garments. This also involved the fashions for different seasons, as it was vital to purchase the right materials, at the right time, and obtain a good stock control for the survival of the business.

It is generally acknowledged that you will make a loss in the first year of any business. I could not afford for this to happen. It was a question of making money, simple as that. I moved into the refurbished flat over the shop, and made a business plan which basically involved opening the shop Monday to Saturday, with half day closing on Wednesday. This half day was need to complete the admin involved in running the shop. Every Sunday I would do my buying, and I have to say the plan worked quite well. Trade in the shop was steady and I was learning fast, basically through my customers, which is the best way to learn. As the business progressed it was very obvious that dress remnants on their own were not enough and I needed to have the accessories that complemented the sale of the materials. I started going to East London wholesalers on a Friday evening to find the best place available to make the right purchases. It was important to go each week to replace stock, to try something new, and steadily build up the stockholding without too much outlay. This meant long hours, however, when you are working for yourself, time doesn't come into it.

I purchased my core stock, dress remnants, from a wholesale outlet in Salford. I had a long drive every Sunday morning. The traffic wasn't too bad considering that at the time there was no M6, and the M1 still only reached the Derby turn off. By going every Sunday, I had the opportunity to purchase in-demand remnants, also the different types of materials, colours, prints and shades. There was a lot involved, especially with me spending my hard earned money.

At this stage, I would like to thank the owner of Bernard Textiles who went out of his way to help me obtain the right stock, and kept back in-demand remnants for me when they became available. This helped me to build up a good range of remnants in the shop which helped to stimulate my cash flow.

By managing to keep changing the materials each week, I kept the customers interested as they were able to purchase the materials they wanted, plus most important it reduced dead stock, remnants that nobody wanted and which tied up my money. I soon found out that selling dress remnants had a high degree of risk. It was also very challenging, but had a good profit margin and there was limited competition, so money was there to be made. After saying that, how do you get customers to venture into a secondary shopping area?

Advertising was very expensive with my limited budget,

and obviously, the best form of advertising is free. With this in mind, I would write to Women's Institutes and other organisations, offering a dress remnant sale at their meetings, and I would give a talk free of charge. The idea was well received and I started selected bookings for evening ladies' group meetings. They were more than happy because they got a free speaker for their meeting. I was happy because I was selling stock and picking up a lot of good ideas on the right materials to buy. At the same time, I was advertising the shop. One of the clubs I attended was a Wednesday afternoon meeting of the Dunstable Townswomen's Guild, with over 100 ladies, for my talk. This produced good sales. I also visited people's homes in the evening which proved to be a great benefit to my business and I acquired a lot of new customers.

As time evolved, the business started building up but I was still not in a position to employ any staff except for a Saturday girl. However, as I've mentioned, when you are self-employed, the hours you work mean nothing.

One evening, I returned from a dress-remnant party in an electric thunderstorm to find my shop flooded. I was told that because of a dip in the road, the drain outside the shop could not cope with the downpour. Luckily my stock was on tables. I just had to clear the water with the help of the fire brigade and dry out the carpets. I opened the next day at the usual time, with just lack of sleep.

Time went on and it was very pleasing to note that the shop takings were rising each week and a good solid customer base was being established, but it was still not enough to sustain a viable business. I will never forget the day when a customer walked into the shop and asked me if I was able to obtain offcuts of fur fabric. I honestly didn't know what they were talking about. Little did I know it would dramatically change the course of my business.

When I next visited the wholesaler, they had a few fur fabric remnants and I made an initial purchase of ten pieces. Then demand started to increase unbelievably over a short period of time. I started selling more fur fabric than dress remnants. This prompted me to consider changing the direction of my business which was a big gamble.

At this point a major opportunity presented itself which required me to put on my best clothes and visit the bank manager. This was to request a further loan, and an increased overdraft facility. The main reason was that I wanted to purchase the freehold of a double fronted shop with a maisonette over it. This had become available in the same parade of shops. My business plan was accepted, knowing full well that if my gamble failed I would be homeless and jobless. It pleased me to have the full backing of the bank manager.

If I could give advice to anybody about the retail business, it would be to listen to your customers. One such was a lady who regularly visited the shop. She was a shopkeeper's dream of a wonderful assistant, very friendly and bags of personality. I offered Audrey a job as a part time assistant. After talking to her husband, she accepted my offer which pleased me very much and I was confident that she would be of great benefit to the business.

Another customer who I admired was an elderly lady who visited the shop on a number of occasions. I found out she was brilliant at designing and making soft toys. My mind started working overtime and soon scaled down the patterns I was buying as she started to design and produce patterns to sell in the shop, thanks to the skill of my valued customer. With the pending move to my new premises, the employment of a part time assistant, and the possible opportunity to expand the business into soft toy making, the future was looking good.

As time went on, I was purchasing more and more fur fabric remnants, and could see that I was creating a specialist market for people making soft toys. It was amazing how the business grew, which meant I was stretched to the limit. On one of my visits to my textile merchant, I had a chat with another shop owner from Manchester who told me where I could obtain fur fabric more cheaply, and from a bigger selection. This was a small mill in Dewsbury, West Yorkshire. I had no idea what was coming. A very important development was the fact that it sold waste fibre. This is the waste from the production of fur fabric which is carded to make it fluffy and is packed into bags of any weight. I soon found out that this was the ideal fibre for filling toys as it was fully washable and flameproof, as well as being nice and fluffy to give the toys a good shape. The only problem was availability. This depended on the amount of fabric sold to create the waste. To try and meet the demand to purchase a good selection of fur fabric and most important the demand for waste fibre, it meant an early start on a Sunday morning to romantic Dewsbury to get there before the mill opened to wholesale customers at 10am.

I also started gradually reducing all the accessories I sold for dressmaking, and started purchasing toy components. This included different types and sizes and colours of eyes, noses, joints and paws, and various other parts, to cater for all the different soft toys my customers were making. I was really amazed at the variety of components available to the customer. If I could give advice to anybody about retail sales, it would be to listen to your customers, you never know how much they may help in promoting the business, like Audrey. I always enjoyed when she visited the shop. Her personality shone out and she was very good at making soft toys. I was so pleased when I was able to offer Audrey employment on a full-time basis. This pleased me very much as the next stage in my business was looming.

Things looked even brighter after a friendly chat with another fellow trader when on one of my regular buying visits. He could not understand why I was travelling all the way to Dewsbury when there was a fur fabric wholesaler in Kent. I immediately made it my business to visit them, and had a chat with the owner. I was very impressed with his range of stock which included offcuts of specialised fabric used for making coats and jackets. These came from a manufacturer where they were made for export. This also meant there was more waste fibre available for filling the toys. They also had a very comprehensive range of toy parts and components. It goes without saying that I never went to the fabric mill at Dewsbury again. I was more than pleased with my new supplier in Sittingbourne. After not too long a period I became a very important customer and I was receiving discounts and given priority on materials in short supply. This was generally making me more money and keeping up my stock levels.

One evening I received a call from Malcolm, the wholesaler in Kent. He told me that a large van had just arrived at his premises full of bags of waste fibre. Unfortunately, he had nowhere to store it and could I take it all? In reality there was no way I could handle a load like that. But I said to him, "send the van up." I rang my mate Tom, who didn't live too far away, to come and help, but warned him he might not get home until late. The large van duly arrived. I opened the back doors and the contents nearly fell out into the road. "Where am I going to put this lot," I thought. Tom and I managed to put some on the land at the rear of the shop and covered it with tarpaulin. The rest we took up to the flat. It filled my bedroom and part of the lounge. I slept in the kitchen and somehow bent around the bags to watch television in the lounge. Before the driver left, he gave me an invoice and from that moment I had achieved my objective which was getting the waste fibre directly from the manufacturers in Folkestone. That meant I got the fibre much more cheaply and in plentiful supply. The next day I visited the council and managed to rent a large storage garage which was situated about half a mile from the shop.

By good fortune and hard work, my dream of having a successful business was taking shape, even though it was very different from when I first started. To summarise: I had bought the freehold of double fronted shop with a maisonette above, I had the monopoly on waste fibre direct from the manufacturer, I had a brilliant shop assistant working with me, and an outworker worth her weight in gold designing soft toy patterns and making them for me.

Purchasing a double fronted shop was one thing, filling it with stock was another. I purchased ten-yard lengths of fur fabric in all colours and rolled them round cardboard tubes to make them look bigger. I bagged up the waste fibre filler into poly bags of different weights and separated the darker from the lighter fillings, so that when making white or light coloured toys, the filling wouldn't show through. I also acquired bags of quality fur fabric offcuts from the manufacturers, plus felt, and components, basically everything for people making soft toys. To keep up with the flow of waste fibre form Folkestone involved hiring a 7.5 tonne cargo van and a visit to Folkestone nearly every week. This involved travelling through London as the M25 didn't exist. It also meant bed and breakfast.

My assistant, Audrey, was soon paying dividends with her lovely way with the customers and knowledge of making soft toys. I approached another customer who was a friend of Audrey. She was able to work part time doing the office work, and also serve in the shop at busy times. With my staff in full swing – the two part timers plus two Saturday girls, I was free to concentrate on building the business and make sure I had a good stock in the shop. I arranged for my outworker to produce patterns of soft toys that were popular at the time. These included Rod Hull's Emu, Kermit the Frog and Fozzie Bear from the Muppets. The patterns were all made as glove puppets. These proved so popular we couldn't produce the patterns fast enough. This meant that the fur fabric, filler, eyes and other components were selling fast too. I asked two further customers if they would produce toys at home to sell in the shop. This made a wonderful window display and encouraged more people in to buy the patterns and all the materials that went with them. It brought extra trade in through people looking at the wonderful window display. Over a period of time, my outworker designed more patterns for me including a small jointed teddy bear, and easy patterns for children who were my future customers.

I registered Equality Soft Toys and employed a further four people who worked from home. I started selling soft toys to car showrooms and other interested companies who bought them for promotional purposes. This was a good example of using my stock to further the business, at the same time employing out-workers with relatively little extra work involved for me.

My next project was a mail order division, which once again was a good way of maximising my existing stock. This proved to be steady, however it was hard to justify the work involved which was mainly packing a distribution. On the plus side, it was instrumental in attracting more customers to the shop. I had a sound viable specialist retail business under the registered name of Equality. I was employing four shop staff and six part-time outworkers. The business progressed well with brilliant staff, good organisation and hard work.

I really admire anybody when they decide to become self-employed. With any business they decide to do it requires hard work and long hours. However, it is very satisfying as you create your own destiny. It took me a while to discover that it was also very important to have an outside interest to take me away from the business for a few hours each week to relax my mind and also to have a social life.

AN UNUSUAL WEDDING

I have always loved football. Due to this, I helped to start a new junior football club, The Tigers. This was to be based in Grove Hill, Hemel Hempstead. My sister Anthea lived there with her husband Chris. They had two sons who loved football as well as a daughter who had no interest at all. The eldest, Darren, was a good goalkeeper and Vince a very good midfield player. I helped with the organisation and running of the club, plus looking after the under 10s team which was the youngest age boys could play in league football. Although we lost every game but one, which we drew, in our first season, the lads enjoyed playing and knew they were up against stiff opposition in a tough league. But before the start of the next season something happened that would completely change my life.

I was informed about a young lad, about nine years old, who had expressed an interest in joining The Tigers. I also heard that he was a very good footballer. He was in the right age group for my team. Because of protocol, we liked to visit their home and speak to the parents and explain the workings of the club and our responsibility to the child while they were in our care. So with agreement from his mum, Eddie joined our team. As time went by, I got to know his mum, Shirley. She would sometimes attend the local games, or on returning Eddie home after an away game, she might invite me in for a cup of tea.

Shirley had been married to a Nigerian man who had tragically died in an accident, so widowed, with three children to bring up, she moved to Grove Hill. Eventually the older two children left the family home. My visits for a cup of tea grew longer as we got to know and understand each other. From then our relationship grew and grew. I would like to say that at this point in my life, aged forty, I had never been married, and never really had a serious girlfriend. But my feelings were changing and Shirley and I began to realise that we loved each other very much.

I remember proposing to Shirley. She did not say yes immediately, but at least she hadn't said a definite no. I realised that she had had a difficult time in her life. Being in a mixed race marriage had its difficulties. This was in the 60s and 70s and it wasn't always accepted. She confided in a close friend about my proposal, someone who had noticed how the relationship was progressing, who told her "not to be silly". So the answer was a definite yes, and we were married six months later at Hemel Hempstead Register Office. It poured with rain all day. The wedding photos had to be taken at the reception which was in Chipperfield, a lovely little village on the edge of Hemel Hempstead. We flew out next day for our honeymoon in Madeira.

HOW I PROGRESSED IN LIFE

I had no further problems with my epilepsy although it was very important that I still took my medication as prescribed. This helped me with my confidence, considering the pressures I had been through over the years of running the business.

My specialist retail business was well established and continued at a manageable rate. But like any other business I was always aware of increased competition. I purchased my core part of the business, fur fabric by the roll, in all colours and was able to buy the toy components and other items in bulk. My weekend trips to Folkestone for the waste fibre were reduced as I rented a large garage from the council for storage. I have to thank my assistant Audrey who was promoted to full time. She was brilliant. The amount of work she covered took a lot of pressure away from me. My travelling was reduced getting the stock. This meant I had more time to enjoy married life, although it was still very hectic.

Having worked hard building up my business, my overall responsibility was now with my wife Shirley and my three stepchildren. Shirley was not the type of person to work in the shop. She managed to help on a part-time basis, and it worked really well. It was a pleasure for me to come home from work to my loving wife after the shop closed. As time progressed at the shop, the novelty of customers making soft toys for resale started to decline. Over a period of time, the soft toys coming in from overseas became much more popular than being locally made here.

In my estimation there is no point trying to save a sinking ship. I had a long discussion with Shirley and the family about what I had in mind. My thoughts were to sell the freehold shop property, and to purchase a corner shop or village store in a suitable location. To say that this was a big decision to make is a huge understatement. However, it received a favourable response. The two children living away from home thought it was a good idea but requested that their mum didn't move too far away. Eddie was quite excited by the thought of living at a shop that sold sweets and other eye-catching edible items. Shirley was in full agreement with the closing of the fur fabric business and the pending change of direction. But obviously the type of property had to be agreed by both of us. This was perfectly understandable, although my thoughts were on a viable business proposition. I looked in the right publication to find suitable properties that were, or about to, come onto the market. I viewed a shop with good accommodation, but I didn't like the idea of the Co-op trading on the other side of the road.

It was proving very difficult to find the right property that would be suitable as both our home and a viable business. However, something always comes along for those who wait, and we found our dream home at a village called Haversham, near Wolverton, and not far from Milton Keynes.

It was a three bedroom detached corner house which included a shop on half the ground floor. All the houses in this area were built in the 1950s to accommodate employees of the local Wolverton Railway Works. This was a very large employer at that time. There was a primary school just opposite the shop. Today these houses are all privately owned. The shop traded as the local convenience store which included being a newsagent with four delivery rounds, and off licence, and a sub-post office. I was able to sell my property at Apsley very quickly with the shop as a going concern. I had my bid accepted for our dream home at Haversham. Moving house is never easy, especially as I had to attend court twice at Milton Keynes to see if I was a suitable person to obtain a licence to sell alcohol. The other tricky part was having to take an exam at Post Office headquarters to see if I had the knowledge to run a sub-post office. Thankfully everything was fine, otherwise I would have been in real trouble. So the move went ahead in September 1988.

One important part of the new business venture which I had to get used to very quickly was the four paper rounds. I had to be up by 5.30 every morning, except Christmas day, to sort out the daily newspapers and magazines that were delivered to the shop about 6am. I also had to have the delivery rounds ready by 7am for the paper boys to deliver. I then opened the shop. The paper rounds were a very important part of the business as this was a guaranteed income and included some customers who had a lot of magazines. At the time, only newsagents sold papers. The sub-post office proved another important part of the shop as it provided a guaranteed income decided by the Post Office. This was based on the previous year's business. Like any other corner shop, business was steady. It was always busy early with people coming in to purchase daily papers and cigarettes. Once the children had gone to school there was a steady stream of mothers buying groceries. The shop was just off the main road. Lorry drivers would park up and pop into the shop for snacks.

As always, if the weather was bad, trade suffered. Having the post office helped to keep the business on an even keel as it brought people into the shop. This was mainly in the morning. Shirley was able to serve in the shop whilst I could concentrate on dealing with post office business.

We had not been trading very long when the government introduced the deeply unpopular "poll tax". This had a serious effect on us as I had to pay for myself and Shirley and on top of that I had to pay business tax for the shop. To overcome this, I worked on increasing the newspaper rounds plus opening the shop for longer in the evenings.

This had a welcome effect of increasing sales at the off licence. I cannot tell you how pleased I was when the government decided that the poll tax wasn't the right system of collection.

There was one particular problem that was really getting on my nerves, which had nothing to do with the business. Outside the door to the shop was a forecourt with a public phone on it. This was below our lounge which was on the first floor. There were no mobile phones in those days. This attracted children in the evening which caused problems and made it very noisy. For the youngsters it was a place to meet. I sent a letter to BT requesting that the phone box be moved to another part of Haversham. Their reply was very positive. They would arrange to remove the phone…but the crunch was that it wouldn't be repositioned. This caused uproar among the residents who convened a meeting but to no avail. BT were able to prove that the only people who used the phone box were people who visited the shop but didn't live in Haversham. This caused a lot of publicity locally which ironically was great for the shop takings.

As time went on, I was very happy how the business progressed. Shirley and I were really enjoying the experience and meeting new people in our corner shop and sub-post office.

Beverley moved to Milton Keynes with her young son,

Tyrone. Eddie went to live with his cultural friends at Hemel Hempstead. Tyrone was Shirley's first grandchild and I got on very well with him. I actually took him at the age of 5 years for a week's holiday at Butlin's, Skegness. I thought this was very brave of me. He really enjoyed the experience and we had a lovely holiday.

We settled into our new life really well despite it being very hectic. Shirley was brilliant when serving in the shop. She could create great conversations with customers, who loved it. I concentrated on the post office which was quite busy. At that time the government benefits were nearly all paid by weekly payments and not through the bank. It was even better when they spent some of their money in the shop. Interestingly, a few people would not use the post office in case somebody overheard how much they were getting. Apparently this is something that happens in village life.

As life went on there always seemed to be something around the corner. At Christmas 1990, Shirley's 85-year-old mother was staying with us for the festive celebration. She was a wonderful lady who always looked after herself. On Boxing Day morning, I took her a cup of tea in bed. Unfortunately, I found she had passed away. It was something I had never experienced in my life, and I never wish to see anything like it again. Obviously, Shirley was deeply hurt and it took some time for her to come to terms with the tragic circumstances. All credit to her for helping me keep the shop running in extremely difficult times.

ABSOLUTELY TERRIBLE

During 1991 it was the start of a deep recession in the country. This pushed up the unemployment rate to well over 3 million and with a staggering 13% interest rate. In the spring of that year, the post office authorities decided to close my sub-post office together with many more all over the country. That was bad enough but there was worse to come. Shirley had been unwell for some time. After numerous tests, we were both shocked to find out she had lung cancer. This came completely out of the blue. As Milton Keynes was being built as a new town, the hospital did not yet have the facilities needed and Shirley was transferred to the care of Northampton General Hospital.

Eventually, I was taking Shirley to Northampton virtually every day. Not being a medical person, I had every hope she would make a full recovery. Being a non-smoker, and only 50, I thought there couldn't be anything serious, although at this point I did know that Shirley would never be the same again. I was having a terrible time coming to terms with the seriousness of her illness, and also the economic problems caused by the closure of the post office, and keeping the shop running.

I was unable to operate the shop as I did not know when I would be able to open and shut. I had no alternative but to put the property – our home and business – on the market. Prospective buyers were slow to view due to the recession that had hit the country. After protracted negotiations I was able to make a sale. The amount I had to agree was nowhere near what I would have liked. Even worse, the shop was never going to open again as the buyer was going to use the shop area for accommodation. This had the effect of my not getting payment for the stock value, or receive any money for the goodwill of the shop and business. My solicitor advised that this was the best offer available, bearing in mind the economic circumstances, and the loss of the post office.

After selling the corner shop, I moved into rented accommodation in Bletchley, Milton Keynes, and was also able to get a temporary job running a newsagent within a pharmacy, which was situated inside a large business building in central Milton Keynes, that housed a number of businesses and office accommodation.

This temporary job lasted six years. At this point, I would like to thank Has Modi, the owner of Jardine's Chemist Group, for his unstinting support and all the time he allowed me to have off work during this very difficult period.

Shirley was an outpatient for a while involving a 35-mile round trip three times a week. She was deteriorating badly. I remember the time a doctor called me into his office to tell me that there was nothing more they were able to do. I do not know how I drove the car home. Shirley was a patient at the Northampton General until she was transferred to Willen Hospice at Milton Keynes. On the second day when I visited Shirley, I took Tyrone, her grandson, with me. He really loved his Nan, and wanted to see her. He was shown into her room. A short while later he came out and said to me, "Nanny is dead." My reply was, "Don't be silly, she's probably just having a sleep." A nurse came quickly and went in to see Shirley. I promptly followed and it was confirmed that Shirley had passed away. I could not believe it would happen on only the second day at the hospice.

Shirley was a very special lady, a terrible loss at only 50 years of age. I am fighting the tears while I write this although it happened over twenty years ago. The staff at the hospice were brilliant looking after Tyrone. At that point I could not cope with what had happened. Later, I was able to contact my sister who worked for a funeral director, and she was able to make all the funeral arrangements. I was not in a position to do anything. I cannot remember how I was able to contact her children. I am a very emotional person and was virtually unable to remember much that happened during the funeral service. I cannot thank my sister Anthea enough for all the arrangements she made and accommodating me at her family home for a while. Whilst staying with my sister, it enabled me to gather my thoughts. The realisation of being widowed, losing my home and my business, was unmanageable. This really tested my inner strength to carry on with life. However, I made the correct decision on returning to my rented accommodation in Bletchley. This was very important as I still had a job of work which involved serving customers and talking to them which helped me to adjust to the loss of my wife and being widowed. I also had a very helpful boss who was of great help to me as was his good wife. I also knew in my mind an unfortunate situation was going to happen when I visited my solicitors. Shirley had not left a will, which I soon discovered caused numerous problems. Let me reiterate. Shirley, who was English, had been widowed through the death of her late Nigerian husband. They had three children, who by now were all over 18 years of age and had been living away from home for a considerable time. The situation was very complex, and even more involved as I was not able to allow one of the children to attend a meeting which was arranged through my solicitor. This was the appropriate way, I thought, that all Shirley's goods and money be distributed in the correct way. This was acceptable to all concerned. It was a very difficult situation but I am pleased to say that everything was concluded so as not to cause any future problems.

Following this traumatic period, and after deep thought and sleepless nights, I made a decision to completely cut myself off from the three stepchildren and grandchildren, and never see them again. What a thing to do! But it was my life. I had lost my loving wife, my home and my business. There is an old saying that "good comes out of bad". I was determined to get my life back on track and be happy.

After six months living at Bletchley, I was given notice to leave my rented house. The owners were coming back to live in their property. This was because they had been living and working at RAF Uxbridge which was to be closed down by the government. It just proves that when you rent a property you never know what might happen. I was able to find more good rental accommodation at Bancroft, Milton Keynes. I was told the property was on a long term let. Funny, that is what the previous one said. At least I had a roof over my head.

TRAVELLING MAN

After two years of widowhood, I felt able to go on holiday on my own. I went to Scotland for a fortnight, by my favourite mode of transport, the railway, who had given me the sack 34 years earlier. I stayed at a lovely B&B in Oban which was at the top of a steep hill. This had a wonderful view over the harbour. What surprised me was the number of people on holiday I spoke to who were also widowed. Obviously it was something I had never thought about in the past.

The following day I decided to go on an organised coach and boat trip to the Isle of Mull and across to the island of Iona. I seated myself with a lady who, unknown to me, was a widow, and travelled by car from Stirling for a day out. We really got on very well together and had a very enjoyable day out which culminated in having a really nice meal at a restaurant near the port of Mull. We then got the late ferry back to Oban.

Unfortunately, I had to say goodbye to my lady friend for that day as she was driving back to her home at Stirling, while my mind was working overtime as I trudged up the hill to my B&B. I spent a further couple of days in Oban. It is a lovely place to visit and I continued my Scottish holiday on the train to Inverness. It was making use of my seven-day rail rover ticket. This allowed me unlimited travel on the trains and ferries in Scotland. I visited the tourist office in Inverness and arranged my accommodation for three nights at another nice B&B next to the river Ness in the city.

The following day I got up early and got a train from inverness to the Kyle of Lochalsh. A wonderful journey on one of the most scenic railway journeys in the world. The Kyle of Lochalsh is a small seaside port which was the point for boarding a ferry on the short journey across the water to the Isle of Skye. Today a bridge crosses from the mainland to the island. I then went by local transport to the main town of Portree which is now a bustling port and a thriving cultural centre. This was different from when I visited which was about twenty years ago.

The Kyle of Lochalsh.

My Amazing Life

Trying to find somewhere to stay that night was proving difficult. The way of life there at the time was totally different. I literally went door knocking on a road that had a few small places with B&B signs, but they were full. I found a house with good Scottish people that were more than happy to put me up for the night. What I didn't bargain for was the lady of the house inviting residents round to see me. I suppose it was my London accent which suddenly made me a celebrity. I was amazed how many of the people had never even been to Glasgow or Edinburgh, let along England. It was like living in another world.

It was a great evening's conversation, especially when the two ladies found out that I was a widower. It was unbelievable. There must have been a shortage of men on the island at that time, but I had no intention of getting married again!

The following day I said goodbye to my island friends and went on an organised coach trip round the beautiful island and returned by ferry to the Kyle of Lochalsh. Then I went on another lovely scenic train journey back to Inverness. I returned to the same accommodation, as the landlady had kindly kept me a room whilst I was on Skye. What lovely Scottish people. The following day I was up early and left Inverness for my journey home. I had a really enjoyable time touring the north of Scotland by my favourite transport. It is really something when you are able to view the wonderful scenery we have in our country from the window of a train. I treated myself to a meal on the train from Glasgow on the way home. There was only one problem: when the train braked suddenly I nearly swallowed my soup spoon. It was a wonderful holiday with lovely weather and did me the world of good.

It was good to be home at my terraced house in Bancroft, which was a nice area of Milton Keynes, with good residents both sides of me. Most important, I had a job to go to which I really enjoyed. There is nothing better than going to work and doing a job you really like. My boss was very interested when he found out that I used to run a post office. He had two chemist's shops in Milton Keynes with sub-post offices in them. When one of these was very busy he would arrange cover for the shop I was in, whilst I was taken to the post office that needed me. I also went for longer periods to cover staff holidays and sickness.

As you may have gathered, I am a very adventurous person and had a perfect opportunity to pursue my love of travelling when my brother David, his wife Christine and three young children emigrated to Canada over thirty years ago. David made a big decision and moved to Calgary, in the state of Alberta, with his job.

On one of my early visits to Calgary I arranged a special

trip for a couple of days. I booked myself on one of the last passenger trains to run from Calgary to Vancouver. The train arrived at in Calgary at 8.00am, having spent the previous two days travelling across Canada from Nova Scotia.

The train proceeded to the lovely town of Banff, and then had to negotiate through the Rocky Mountains. Part of this was via a major feat of engineering called Kicking Horse Pass, where two spiral tunnels were built to get the trains through, and it's an amazing sight.

Today there is a vantage point high up beside the road where people can see the very long freight trains winding their way through the spiral tunnels. When the front of the train is out of the tunnel, you can still see the back of it disappearing into the mountain.

The train went along at a slow pace for miles, stopping only once for a black bear, which was having a sleep on the railway line. You do not try and mess with a black bear unless you are mad.

After a few hours, we arrived in Kamloops, a large city where there is also an Indian Reservation. We continued to Vancouver in the early morning when it was still dark, as some passengers were terrified by the sheer drop to the sea if they could see it.

When I arrived in Vancouver, I took a passenger boat to Vancouver Island and enjoyed a wonderful day. It was a bit like England with red buses. I travelled to the centre of the island, and then got a passenger boat back to north Vancouver. After that, I got a taxi to the railway station for the evening train back to Calgary which left after darkness had fallen.

I visited the observation coach at the rear of the train and had a nice chat with a lad there who was going home to Kamloops after studying to be a plumber. He told me that was a native American. An elderly man interrupted, another native American, but he did not like my conversation for some reason, and became aggressive. Brian left the observation coach toot quick!

After travelling back through Kamloops and Kicking Horse Pass again, my journey ended when the train arrived back at Calgary in the early morning. That was a trip never to be forgotten.

It really goes without saying that I never knew what was going to happen next in my life. I will always remember coming home from work one evening which happened to be my birthday, the 30th December. I was 54 years of age. Nothing had been arranged, just another year gone by and getting used to running a home on my own, or so I thought.

I finished work a bit late and drove the couple of miles home. When I parked outside my house I noticed a lady standing by the side of the road. She politely said she was waiting for a taxi which had not turned up. I asked her where she was going and she told me to a bingo evening in Milton Keynes. I told her not to worry about a taxi, I would give her a lift. She was a nice friendly lady and accepted my offer. I also said a few kind words and arranged to collect her after the bingo and take her home. It did make me think how a nice mature lady would allow a stranger to take her to bingo in his car, and then allow me to collect and take her home. I soon found out the answer. I remember saying to her on the way to bingo, "You are very honoured tonight." She asked me why. "Because it is my birthday today," I replied. This started a longer conversation. The lady's name was Doreen and she had been widowed for three years. She said, "you may be surprised but I know you." My reply? "Know me? You're having a laugh!"

Doreen had not known me to speak to, but had been spying on me from her home. This was a semi-detached property opposite to mine. At that point I remembered seeing her a couple of times, but we hadn't spoken. I probably thought her husband was inside the house. From then on we had good conversations whilst driving, which made me suddenly realise I was taking her to bingo. When I collected Doreen that evening she had not won a penny. But I had wondered a lot when she invited me to her home the following evening which was New Year's Eve.

Just as my life evolved, a normal birthday suddenly became a very interesting birthday. As mentioned, Doreen invited me across the road to her home for New Year's evening. She arranged to phone me when it was time to come over so I immediately gave her my phone number. Doreen was a lovely lady, really down to earth and a great conversationalist. We saw in the New Year together and we really enjoyed each other's company. She worked part time as a caretaker at the local meeting hall on the estate and had made a number of good friends with the ladies. I did not see Doreen as much as I would have liked. Obviously I had a job that kept me busy. Also, she would have her friends round just about every day.

Doreen had moved to Milton Keynes from Plymouth, where she was born. Her family members still lived there except her daughter and a son, Kevin, who moved from Plymouth and lived with his partner in Newport Pagnell. He was a self-employed tree surgeon and did very well. Doreen was very loyal to her friends who were very conscious of me getting in her way. Plus, there was Kevin, who was a really nice man, but what I would call a "mummy's boy". It was understandable that after losing his father, he definitely didn't want his mother getting mixed up with any other man. However, the daughter was quite happy for her mum to see me. I remember her saying, "my mother is not stupid; she will soon tell you where to go if anything is not right for her." She never visited my house. Being a loyal person, she did not want to upset her friends and she certainly did not want Kevin to see his mum in my home.

Despite the difficult circumstances, we were able to see each other quite a lot, as very good friends. We just had to be careful, to say the least. I enjoyed my new rented accommodation and my job was going well. Then just as I was getting really settled into my life, Doreen let me know that she had talked to her daughter and arranged to move and live with her at Woburn Sands. Thinking about it, I suppose it was the logical thing to do financially. Plus, the fact was that her daughter was a single mum with two children. I saw her a couple of times after she moved, but the circumstances were not right and we wished each other all the very best in our lives with health and happiness.

It is always nice when you enjoy going to work. This was the case working at one of the Jardine Group shops, which was a chemist and newsagent at the Central Business Exchange in Milton Keynes. It was also nice occasionally having a change, helping out at their sub-post offices when needed. However, another job opportunity was presented to me. Because of my experience running a convenience store and news agency, I was offered and accepted the position of Relief Manager for the One Stop Shop group, covering their shops within a 25-mile radius of Milton Keynes. This included a better salary and a mileage allowance. Basically, I covered their shops that were without a manager, but in the main when the company were short of managers at their shops because of sickness and holidays.

The One Stop group had a large number of shops in Milton Keynes. The population was growing all the time and progressing over 300k. There was a shop on nearly every estate. This was one of the reasons that attracted me to work for the company. I settled into my new job very well managing shops mainly in Milton Keynes. It was hard work, but not too bad if you had your head screwed on, and quite often very long hours. This did not bother me too much as I did not have anybody to go home to, a bit sad. One of the things about any shop on an estate, it attracts a mixture of good and dodgy customers plus some unwanted visitors. It was also a haven for children. If the kids want to meet on an evening, you can bet your bottom dollar that they will arrange to meet outside the shop.

A lot of things have happened to me over the course of a few years. I will just mention a couple of instances. One day, two men walked into the shop and started helping themselves to alcohol from the off licence area. I was serving behind the counter at the time. My lady assistant came out of the office and tried to stop them. The men left the shop, their arms loaded with spirits. My assistant then made a big mistake. She went after them not knowing there was a third man waiting outside who knocked her to the ground. She was injured and off work for a month. I was all right in this instance, but had to extend my stay at the shop, working seven days a week for a month.

Another incident happened one evening when some older children were playing outside the shop with a football. It was a nice evening and the shop door was open. One lad kicked the football into the shop which hit an elderly lady who was looking at the magazines on the rack. Thankfully the lady was all right. I picked the football up and took it to my office. A teenager followed me requesting to have his ball back. He tried to enter my office. I just put my hand on his chest, gave him a push so I could shut the office door and stop him entering. My intention was to take the ball into my office as evidence because I was going to call the police as I knew the boy was a well-known troublemaker and I had an elderly customer who was very shaken up.

Then I got a shock. A police officer visited my shop to question me on an assault charge. The boy's father had contacted the police exaggerating what I had done, and wanting to press charges. We were interviewed at the local police station and all charges were dropped. It just goes to prove how careful any person in responsibility has to be when dealing with the general public.

Life has strange twists; you never know what might happen. I had a phone call one day from head office asking if would be able to manage on of their shops at Henley on Thames for three months, knowing it was outside the area of my agreed employment. I was quite happy for a change, and Henley seemed the ideal place. The only unfortunate part was that it was during the winter. However, it worked out really well. I lived there five days a week. The company paid for my full board at a private residence, and I would return to my home for the weekend. In that sort of job, having Saturday and Sunday off was unheard of so everything worked out fine. It was a nice shop, smaller than I had been used to. There were some very friendly customers, even television stars, certainly different to what I was used to. My only problem occurred if a newspaper delivery boy or girl didn't turn up for their round, and I would have to do the delivery. At that time, nearly everybody had newspapers delivered and they were not small ones. Half the time I didn't know where I was going but it all worked out. A couple of residents put me right in no uncertain terms.

It is a known fact that if you do a really good job for your employer, you are pushed into doing more work, whatever form it may take. After my stint at Henley, the One Stop Shop group started sending me to places way outside the area I was originally asked to cover. This involved a lot of travelling and getting home very late at night. Plus, more often than not, sorting out the mess at a shop left behind by the previous manager. It was unbelievable, the work I was asked to do sometimes.

One day, when I arrived home from work quite late, I looked at my mail before I went to bed. Normally I was too tired to concentrate on opening the mail. I would leave it until the next morning. Something in my mind that night told me to open a letter. It looked very official.

The letter was from my landlords, and they were giving me two months' statutory notice to leave my house. My heart sank. I had been living there for nearly six years, a long time in a rented property. Obviously I had looked after it as though it were my own home and over the years as a tenant I didn't think the notice would ever happen. The reason for the notice to quit was due to circumstances beyond their control. They had to sell the house. This gave me two months to arrange alternative accommodation and I wasn't thrilled at the thought of moving once again.

At this point, I was 58 years of age, and in good health. The only problem I had was with my epilepsy. Nothing had happened of any significance for over 30 years, as long as I took my medication. If I missed a couple of days, my mind would soon let me know.

Finding a place to rent in Milton Keynes proved very difficult as most houses had excessive rents. This was because of the great job opportunities with companies relocating to there. Plus, it was a very easy commute to London for the many people who worked in the city.

One day, I was reading the local newspaper and was interested in an advert from the Sheltered Housing Association. I wondered what on earth was sheltered housing. I had never heard of it, and nearly ignored the advert but thought better of it and decided to ring the phone number. The lady who answered was very informative and answered a lot of my questions, including about the word "sheltered" which to me suggested "in need of help". Arrangements were made for the lady to visit me. There were 28 sheltered housing units, averaging about 30 flats in each unit. They were all run by the council. The only stipulation was that the person or persons had to be over 50 years old, and it did not matter if they were still working.

Well, I couldn't believe it when I was informed that there were a number of vacancies at different places. I visited Pritchard Court, an older building at Great Linford village, on the edge of Milton Keynes. I fell in love with the place and didn't bother looking anywhere else. I was offered a really nice good sized flat on the first floor. There were communal gardens around the building, and a free laundry room (with times allocated). It had a lovely large lounge where the residents were able to enjoy good conversation and the activities available. It even had an allotment which really pleased me as I love gardening.

I moved in, and settled well. I soon got to know some of the residents, and I was made very welcome, although I was still working long hours. I do remember one day I visited the large indoor shopping centre in Milton Keynes. I looked through the window at one of the shops and thought I recognised someone inside the shop. When the lady turned around I saw it was Doreen. We spoke, and I took her to nice eating place for a drink and a chat. Unbelievably, Doreen was now living in sheltered housing about three miles from my new home. Apparently things did not work out for her living with her daughter. I arranged to meet her one day at her flat, although she was worried about other residents seeing me there. Doreen was a very bubbly and well-liked lady and she had many good friends. It was not my intention whatever to pull her apart from the neighbours, but just to be good friends.

Things moved along and I was leading a really hectic lifestyle, seeing Doreen, making new friends where I lived, and still being a relief manager for One Stop Shops, which involved a lot of travelling. After a lot of thought, I made the decision to leave my job. The amount of travelling I was doing, to and from the shops, was getting too much. It was also causing problems at my home. The company policy was to open all stores until 11pm. If I had to do a late shift, which was quite often, after locking up sometimes I was not getting home until well after midnight. This caused problems getting into my sheltered housing complex, which was understandable for the security of the residents, and I had no wish to disturb anyone.

It is very important that when anybody gives their notice in at their place of employment, they have another job to commence. Even at 62 years of age, I managed to get another job locally to see out my working life. This was as a gate house security officer. It was a twelve-hour shift, four days on and four days off, on a rota system and working nights. This meant one of my shifts would be Monday to Thursday, and the next Tuesday to Friday. Having rarely had a weekend off in my working life for nearly forty years, this was wonderful news. I have to say, I hated the job. But by working out my sleeping patterns I had quite a lot of time off. This enabled me to spend time with my new found friends, despite the odd working days I was doing.

I continued occasionally to see Doreen. This included sometimes driving her to her daughters where at times she also looked after her grandchildren. I also enjoyed working in her daughter's garden.

Life at my sheltered housing complex was getting very

interesting. I was taking two or three ladies for a nice day out in my car. We went to places of interest where they had never been before. We all really enjoyed our days out. The ladies really enjoyed the days as like me they were living alone but got on really well. It got to the point, who do I take next? Once others in the complex heard of these outings they were asking to be included, and a little list was forming. One of the trips was an organised day excursion by train. We left Northampton at 7am to, believe it or not, the city of Glasgow. I love train journeys, speeding along through our wonderful countryside. We arrived in Glasgow at 1.20pm. My instructions to the ladies – stick with me at all times. We walked outside the station and looked for a bar or restaurant to get something to eat. As we walked along the road a large band went past. Most of the people were dressed up following behind. We did find a nice place to eat, and afterwards I enquired where the open top bus tour left from. It was not too far away on the other side of a large city square. To get to the square we had to make our way through all these people who we had previously seen marching along the road behind the band. We found out it was a gay pride rally. However, I didn't know any other way to the bus stop. We went on our open top bus tour which was a very good way of seeing something of Glasgow in a short space of time.

After the trip we alighted from the bus at the central railway station. We had time to have a cup of tea and something to eat before our train left at 6.30.   We had a really good journey back to Northampton. Everybody had a sleep, except me.   On reaching our destination, we travelled back in my car. We all crept indoors at 1.00am. Although I was really pleased that everything had gone so well, I had to think what on earth was I doing?

I have always been a bit dubious about the words "sheltered housing". There must be a better wording. It conjures up all kinds of thoughts in mind like homeless, desperate people needing help or sleeping under a pier at the seaside.   Then my sister put me right.   My mother lived in sheltered accommodation a number of years ago. I just thought it was another flat in a large building at the time. After these thoughts, "sheltered housing" went out of the window, unless someone asked me where I lived. My home was a lovely place and I got to know some really nice people.

There was one lady I got to know quite well. Her name was Marya.   She had been on a couple of my trips, including a five-day coach holiday. Marya was a quiet unassuming lady who enjoyed going on my trips out. I started visiting her in her flat a couple of evenings a week. She was happy to see me but not for too long. Marya had lost her husband a number of years before and her only son was tragically killed in a road accident ten years earlier. I felt really sorry for her. She was a lovely lady who was having a really unhappy life at the time which really affected her way of living. She was a very friendly person but kept herself to herself. However, we got on very well as good friends. Sheltered housing had given me a new lease of life. Everything was going really well. Doreen lived just three miles away. Marya lived just down the corridor. I was making more good friends.

A huge part of anybody's life was fast approaching for me – retirement. This is always a very difficult time for anybody to adjust to. Little did I know there were going to be some dramatic changes that would completely alter my life, and make me a different person.

RETIREMENT

I retired from work on my 65th birthday. At that time, companies were not obliged to extend a person's employment if they didn't wish to do so, not that I was interested in working on any further. I am very proud of the fact that I worked my full 50 years, employed and self-employed. I had a job for the full period without being unemployed or receiving a penny in government benefits.

To celebrate my retirement, I decided to have a special holiday which would only be in keeping with my taste of adventure. Not many people like going on holiday on their own. It is always a chance who you might meet that makes a holiday special, or not so good. I was aware Marya was approaching her 70th birthday with nothing arranged. However, I could not imagine she would consider going on a special holiday with me. I had a good chat with her about us possibly going on holiday together. I also discussed my thoughts on where I was thinking of going. Not somewhere just around the corner. Marya was a very quiet lady, and I have to say, I was shocked when she agreed to come on holiday with me. She insisted on paying her own way, but leaving me to do the organising. We both agreed not to consider England, but chose the communist state of Cuba. I arranged everything through Saga. Part of their group specialises in arranging holidays for the over 50s. Our holiday caused a few eyebrows to flutter among residents at our housing complex. The nosy residents would have had a field day.

We were booked on a flight from Heathrow to Havana, Cuba, with Virgin Atlantic. We were greeted by our coach and courier for the next two weeks' holiday. She told us a lot of interesting facts on how Cuba, a communist country, worked. It was a real adventure. This was in 2006. Whilst driving from the airport to Havana, it ws very evident that Cuba was a very poor country compared to what we were used to.

On entering the city, we went past one large building which looked like a corrugated shack. It was the local hospital! We were staying in a hotel in Havana for the first week. From here we went out for the day, visiting towns and places of interest. It was like going back to the dark ages. I would never have believed people lived in such conditions and the way of life. Yet the people appeared to be healthy and very happy.

Whilst travelling along the open road there was one thing that really interested me. When we passed a junction on the road with no houses around, there were still always people there on the side of the road, if you could call it a road. I asked our courier about this and she confirmed that there was very little public transport outside Havana. Apparently all cars had to stop and give people a lift if they had room. One day, on our travels, I actually saw a lot of people standing on the back of a lorry with sides.

The second part of our holiday was in an all-inclusive five-day stay at a hotel on the other side of the island next to the sea. This had its own private beach. There were four hotels at this resort built by the Spanish. This was a very valuable source of income and employment for the country.

When they said "all inclusive" they meant what they said. I went to the booking office at the hotel and arranged for a Chinese meal at a restaurant about a mile away in a wonderful setting. It was a lovely meal, especially when it was free. It was not the time of the year for the beach, but we enjoyed a nice walk along the beach and on the way back a drink with something to eat, dare I say it, free of charge. The facilities in and around the hotel were second to none, which included a free bus to the nearest town.

It was wonderful holiday. I saw so much that I didn't realise existed in this world. I am so thankful I live in a democratic state and not a communist one. I would like to thank Marya for coming with me. It would not have been the same without her. We had a difficult flight home when the aircraft was diverted because of a very bad storm in the ocean. After my wonderful retirement holiday, which I will never forget, the icing on the cake was the fact that I didn't have to go back to work on the

Monday.

I now had to get back to earth with a bang. I have known people to lose their way in life after retirement. I was going to make sure it did not happen to me. After making enquiries I became a volunteer ranger for the local parks trust. This was a charity that looked after all the woods, lakes, rivers and open spaces in Milton Keynes.

My job was to walk around a chosen area with my rally board and to report back to the office anything that needed attention. This included such things as dangerous pathways, waste, and litter, braches broken from trees, signs damaged, general vandalism, and a lot more. I even went to a gated wood where a dog had been locked in all night and was going mad. I got out very quickly, locked the gate and phoned my office using my mobile, which obviously we had to have.

I did this for a couple of years whenever I wanted. It was very interesting. I never knew what area I was going to, or what I might find. It kept me fit and my brain ticking. On Wednesday mornings for a few weeks I was asked to help out in a small wood. This was being cleared and paths made for the general public to enjoy walking through. The entrance at one end was down a steep slope which needed steps made, with railings. The Parks Trust contacted the appropriate authorities to arrange for supervised prisoners to do the work. The authorities refused the request unless a mobile toilet was provided. The following Wednesday, I went to help at the wood. Just as I got there a lorry pulled up with the delivery of a mobile toilet. I did my voluntary work and went for a pee behind a tree. While the prisoners were taken to the local pub at lunchtime, I had my sandwiches in the wood. I have to say, the prisoners did a good job and I wished them well for the future.

Before I finished my voluntary work for the Parks Trust, I decided to put my name forward to be a parish councillor for my ward, which was Great Linford. This made it four nominations for two positions, one of whom was the standing councillor. The local residents were asked to vote on their ballot form when they were voting for their local councillor at the polling station. I filled in the forms as required beforehand, which included making a statement about myself.

I didn't have a chance of being elected as not many people knew me, except in my housing complex. There are over forty Parish Council wards in Milton Keynes. When the returning officer came to the Great Linford results, I came second and was duly elected for the ward. I have to say, when the result was announced, I couldn't believe it. It was like becoming an MP.

There were fourteen members on the Parish Council. This covered a large area with about 10,000 residents. I attended the main meetings plus additional meetings for allotments and recreation. This also included arranging two large outdoor events during the school summer holidays which I really enjoyed and which kept me busy. I still made time to take the ladies out for the day. I enjoyed good conversation with Marya and also my visits to see Doreen. It was certainly busier than going to work.

If that was not enough, I was elected as Chairman of the Social Club at our sheltered accommodation at Pritchard Court. We had a very good committee and arranged lots of social events with guest speakers plus really good outings. It cost the residents a minimum charge of £1 a week, and included a fish and chip supper once a month. After a couple of years, I had to give my resignation to the parish council as I had to wear a hearing aid, and the building where the parish council met did not have a loop system. The loop system makes conversations much easier for the hard of hearing. Unfortunately, it was getting rather embarrassing at meetings and making it difficult for me to make any contribution to the meeting. Since leaving the parish council, I have taken steps to relieve the problem.

Without any outside voluntary work, I was enjoying my time in my sheltered accommodation. I especially enjoyed helping to make a very vibrant social club for the residents. At the beginning of my 68th year, I made sure I relaxed and enjoyed a peaceful life with wonderful people in lovely surroundings at Great Linford. However, I must have been joking if I knew what was coming next.

I was enjoying my life living in my one-bedroom flat on the first floor of the building. It came to my notice that a ground floor flat became available. It was at one end of the building facing the front. It was number 13, unlucky for some, but was it unlucky for me? I got in touch with the council and asked for a transfer. I thought the ground floor flats might be more for people with some kind of disability but the council did not think that way, and granted my transfer request. It transpired that the lady living in this flat requested to move to the flat opposite as the bathroom facilities were more suitable for her. This person was a really nice lady called Jeanette. She had been a widow for three years, and did not enjoy the best of health. She spent a lot of time staying with her brothers and sisters in Norfolk. This is one reason I had never had the pleasure of meeting Jeanette before. The move went very well and I quickly settled into my new flat. It also enabled me to keep an eye on my car. A lady resident in her late eighties put my curtains up for me. Thank you to "high kicking Doris" an amazing lady.

One of my favourite pastimes that I really enjoy is gardening. I had a large plot about half a mile away at a secure council allotment. I grew vegetables and also had a few fruit bushes. The residents loved it when I was bringing home fresh runner beans, and a lady made jam from the fruit. Having a key to the allotment gate was a wonderful feeling. I could visit there whenever I wanted to for peace and quiet to enjoy my hobby. I also got involved in doing some gardening in the communal area around our flats. There was a greenhouse too. The ground floor flats had a small front garden and I was happy to help residents keep them looking really nice.

One of the things I started doing was growing small plug plants in trays. This is an easier way than growing plants from seed. I put the trays in front of my patio window on the floor in the lounge of my flat and also on the window sill in the corridor. This was all very nice but I forgot I was going away for a week's holiday with my good friend Marya, and the plants needed watering. There was one person who I could trust and would keep an eye and water the plants for me but I was going on holiday with her.

This left me in a quandary. I thought hard, and decided to ask Jeanette who now lived opposite me if she would kindly go into the flat and water all the plug plants for me. She looked a very trustworthy lady. Thankfully she agreed to keep an eye on the plants each day. On returning from holiday I thanked Jeanette and gave her a little present. She seemed a really nice friendly lady. Over the next few weeks I would chat to her quite a lot. We saw each other at the social events and coffee mornings. She asked me to dinner at her flat and I complimented it when I took her out to a restaurant a week later. This was very regular and it included inviting me to her flat for breakfast every day. I could not get out of bed quickly enough. We enjoyed each other's company and we became very good friends. Jeanette enjoyed a very close family with her three sons, seven grandchildren and three great grandchildren. I was lucky enough to get on really well with all the family members.

Another very interesting fact is that Jeanette was a Christian, and had attended the Baptist Church in Bletchley for over 40 years. She had been involved in all aspects of the Church, from decorating to taking Bible classes. Living at our sheltered housing, Jeanette was ten miles from her Church. A member would come in her car and take her to Church every Sunday. My thoughts were to take Jeanette to Church which would save the Church member four journeys.

Our relationship grew very strong. I remember going to my flat, going to bed and realising that at the age of 69 I was madly in love again. Jeanette was a very strong willed lady. She was 76 years of age and kept herself very active. She was not the type of person to make rash decisions and had been widowed for less than two years. As time progressed I got to know her family very well. I would take two of the grandchildren to their chosen sports which they enjoyed. I took Brooke to gymnastics and with her brother Bradley we went to football training. This also included going to the games on match days.

Needless to say, I was also involved in gardening as well.

The fact that Jeanette was a devoted Christian and I was finding my way in the Christian Church meant we never thought about living together. It was not the right thing to do. However, how it happened neither of us really knew, we decided to get married. I didn't even propose to her. All the family were really pleased, although it must have been quite a shock to say the least, to her three sons with their mother deciding to get married again at the ripe old age of 77. This also caused a lot of excitement at our sheltered housing.

I would like to thank Jeanette's sons, Kevin, Christopher and Peter, they were brilliant, and I will do everything in my power to give their mother a wonderful life with health and happiness. When we were arranging our wedding, we had no intention of doing anything special, just a simple wedding. However, members of the family had other ideas. With myself at the age of 70, and Jeanette 77, we were married at our Church, the Spurgeon Baptist Church in Bletchley on Saturday 17th September 2011. We had five bridesmaids from both sides of the family. They were all dressed in outfits and accessories bought in China by son Kevin and his wife Sue, who were working in that country at the time. You can imagine, the bridesmaids looked fantastic. Jeanette looked lovely and radiant as she entered the Church, given away by her son Peter. I was very honoured to have my brother David as my best man. He had come with his wife Christine from their home in Calgary, Canada.

I would like to thank the minister, Chris Bell, who conducted the service to a packed Church. Our reception was held in the adjoining Church hall. After the emotional speeches there was a chance for my side of the family to meet Jeanette's ever growing family. It was a pleasure to see everyone getting on so well together. I would like to thank all the Church members who made our day so special. This included taking the wedding photographs, preparing the Church for the service including all the lovely flower arrangements, not least of all the hard work in setting up and arranging a wonderful buffet reception.

With our minister, Chris Bell.

My Amazing Life

We left for our honeymoon in Somerset with our first night at a village location. We stayed at a lovely guest house in the middle of nowhere. We had lovely walks and also visited some really nice places in Somerset and Devon. I even managed a trip on one of my favourite heritage railways, the West Somerset Railway, which we both really enjoyed.

On returning home, we arranged a party for all our neighbours in our housing complex, with a suitable cabaret. Everybody had a very enjoyable afternoon. A few days later we visited Jeanette's brothers and sisters at Bradwell in Norfolk. We also visited my wife's blind sister Sylvia at Hornchurch in Essex. Words cannot describe how I feel for Sylvia; she is an amazing lady. We are all very lucky in having our sight and hearing.

Getting used to married life again was not very difficult as I had a very special wife and a wonderful family behind me. No way did I wish to be called a stepfather though. My name is Brian and that is what everybody calls me. This was the start of another special part of my life. Could anything else happen?

A REAL RETIREMENT

We settled down to our life together in our flat at the sheltered housing. The building had thirty flats on the ground and first floor. It is important to adjust to such living arrangements as everybody is different. But realistically we were all living together. A warden attended Monday to Friday who visited everybody and helped to sort out any problems, and make life easier for some of the more vulnerable residents who were not so active.

We also enjoyed being able to attend Church every Sunday, and being involved in Church meetings and activities whenever we were able to. I gradually learned more about what being a Christian meant, and realised that although I did believe in God I now personally knew him as my Lord and saviour. At this point I would like to say a big thank you to all the wonderful Christians at Spurgeon Baptist Church who were such an inspiration to me and made feel so welcome.

It was quite a coincidence that I was baptised at our Church exactly one year after we were married there. I cannot honestly describe to you the feelings during my baptism. When I gave my very emotional testimony to the congregation, it was straight from the heart, and affected many people in the Church.

As time progressed we were living a very active and full life, with all the social club commitments, and many other activities within the family, which also involved visiting Jeanette's brothers and sisters in Norfolk. We also enjoyed lovely walks in the area, with walks along the canal towpath, which made it really nice. We were very fortunate living in a village on the edge of Milton Keynes.

Baptism.

However, we were not getting any younger and felt we needed our independence more to enjoy our married life. We visited Bradwell in Norfolk for a short while after a very unhappy event happened when Jeanette's brother Barry died after a very long illness. Barry was a wonderful man. It was very unfortunate that I was only able to meet him on a few occasions. After attending the funeral and talking a lot to Jeanette's brother Billy, sisters and friends, we decided that if an opportunity was presented to us we might consider a move to Norfolk. For Jeanette this was like going home as she was born and brought up in a village called Burgh Castle which is three miles from Great Yarmouth and five miles from Lowestoft. I started making enquiries through the internet, looking for a bungalow to rent which was unfurnished and had a long let. We looked at one such bungalow at Hopton near Lowestoft. We felt we didn't like the surrounding area where the property was situated.

We were not in a hurry to move and were happy to bide our time for the right property to come available. We visited local estate agents and made numerous enquiries. It was not easy trying to rent a property 125 miles away from home. Thanks to the internet, a bungalow came on the market that ticked all the boxes, situated in Bradwell, Norfolk. We arranged for a viewing. It was just the bungalow we were dreaming of, even better than the description on the internet. We signed contracts on the same day, and made our big move on October 25th 2013. The build up to the move went really well. My only slight concern was that the removal van was going to be outside at the time agreed. In keeping with how well the move was organised, the removal van arrived half an hour early. The removal men really worked hard. We could not have wished for a more efficient move to our new home and our new life.

AFTERWORD

I have really enjoyed writing about the story of my life. It is two years now since we moved to Bradwell. Jeanette and I are very happy living in our lovely two-bedroom bungalow in a really nice area with good neighbours. We are close to all amenities including a Baptist Church where we are members and have made really good friends.

Last year was very special for Jeanette who was 80 years old, a remarkable lady. I organised a special event at the local golf club, which was large enough to accommodate our family and close relations. There were over sixty people there and we had a wonderful day.

We have also had some marvellous days out in both Norfolk and Suffolk. You cannot beat walking along Gorleston seafront watching the ships going in and out of the harbour. Total revitalisation, with the sea air keeping you fresh as a daisy.

I hope you have enjoyed reading my book as much as I have loved writing it. As I have experienced, you never know what might happen in life, whether it is good or bad. If there is anything I could recommend, it would be to never give up, always talk to people, and visit your local Church.

Brian Williams 2016

18042097R00055

Printed in Great Britain
by Amazon